Rugby Jokes
in the Locker Room

Rugby Jokes in the Locker Room

Illustrated by
Raymond Turvey

SPHERE BOOKS LIMITED

A *Sphere* Book

First published in Great Britain in 1991 by
Sphere Books Ltd
Reprinted 1991

ISBN 0 7474 0729 0

Printed and bound in Great Britain by
Cox & Wyman Ltd, Reading

Sphere Books Ltd
A Division of
Macdonald & Co (Publishers) Ltd
165 Great Dover Street
London SE1 4YA
A member of Maxwell Macmillan Publishing Corporation

Contents

Office Etiquette
1

Notices Strike Back
47

Bible Belt
83

Good ol' Sex
107

Homework
129

Celebrations!
145

Office
Etiquette

REMEMBER!

The boss is not always right but he's always the BOSS!

CAN YOU PASS THIS TEST?

Have a pencil ready. Maximum time allowed: two minutes.

1. First check the time, then read all instructions carefully before proceeding with the test.

2. Write your name here. _____

3. If your first name has more than four letters, circle it.

4. Draw a triangle here. _____ _____

5. If your first name has four letters or less, place a dot in the triangle.

6. Draw a circle here. _____

7. If you placed a dot in the triangle, draw a line through your name and place an X in the circle.

8. Write the name of a colour here. _____

9. If the colour you wrote was not purple, brown or pink, write your surname here. _____

10. If you wrote your surname, circle it unless it starts with a vowel.

11. If you did not write your surname, write your first name again here. _____

12. Draw another triangle after instruction 4.

13. Write the figure five in the second triangle, unless you placed a dot in the first one.

14. Disregard instructions 2–13 inclusive. Nothing is to be written or drawn anywhere on the test.

15. You pass if you got this far without writing or drawing anything.

If you failed it is because you did not pay attention to instruction 1, which told you explicitly to read all instructions carefully before proceeding.

NOTICE

It has come to the attention of the Management that employees have been dying on the job, either refusing, or neglecting to fall over. This practice must cease forthwith; any employee found dead on the job in an upright position will immediately be dropped from the payroll.

In future, Managers noticing that any employee has made no movement for a period of two hours or more, are asked to investigate, as it is almost impossible to distinguish between death and the natural movement of some employees. Managers are cautioned to make a careful test, such as holding a paypacket in front of the suspected corpse. Care should be exercised however, with the paypacket, as there have been cases where the natural instinct is so deeply ingrained that the hand of the corpse has made spasmodic clutching movements, even after rigor mortis has set in.

I'M A SILENT SALESMAN
Any chance of crawling into bed
with you tonight?

If so, keep this card,

If not . . . kindly return it,
as they are expensive.

P.S. — You don't have to say "yes" . . . just smile.

I am a bit of a BULLSHITTER myself
but it is indeed a pleasure to
encounter a REAL EXPERT!
— Please Continue

If You're In The Mood For SEX
KEEP THIS CARD AND SMILE

If You're Not In The Mood
TEAR THIS CARD UP.

OUR
WORKING SCHEDULE

Starting Time .... 8.00 a.m.

Morning Coffee Break ..... 9.00–11.30 a.m.

Lunch Hour .... 11.30 a.m.–1.30 p.m.

Afternoon Coffee Break .... 2.00–4.30 p.m.

Quitting Hour .... 5.00 p.m.

WOULD YOU BE VERY UPSET IF I ASKED YOU TO TAKE YOUR SILLY-ASSED PROBLEM DOWN THE HALL ??

PLEASE
DO NOT GO HOME
ON YOUR
COFFEE BREAK!

REMEMBER
WHEN YOU ARE
AT THE END
OF YOUR ROPE,
TIE A KNOT
IN IT
AND
HANG ON

Please do not
Annoy, Torment, Pester,
Plague, Molest, Worry,
Badger, Harry, Harass,
Heckle, Persecute, Irk,
Bully, Vex, Disquiet,
Grate, Beset, Bother,
Tease, Nettle, Tantalize,
or Ruffle the CHAIRMAN

Getting Something Done Around Here is like Mating Elephants

1. It's done at a high level.
2. It's accomplished with a great deal of roaring and screaming.
3. It takes two years to produce results.

NOTICE OF INCREASE IN TAX PAYMENT
EFFECTIVE 1 JUNE 1991
TO ALL MALE TAXPAYERS

Gentlemen,

The only thing the present Government has not taxed is your John Thomas. Mainly because 98 per cent of the time your John Thomas is out of work and the other 2 per cent it is in the hole. Moreover, it has two dependants who are both nuts.

Accordingly, beginning 1 June, your John Thomas will be taxed according to its size, using the John Thomas Chart list below to determine your category. Please insert the information on Page 1, Section F, Line B, of your Inland Revenue Franchise Tax Form.

Sincerely,

JOCK STRAPP

H.M. Inspector

10–12 inches .... Luxury Tax
8–10 inches .... Pole Tax
6–8 inches .... Privilege Tax
4–6 inches .... Nuisance Tax

Note:–

Anyone under four inches is eligible for a refund.

Please do not request an extension.

Males exceeding twelve inches should file under Capital Gains.

INFORMATION TO BE INSERTED ....

WHY WORRY?

There are only two things to worry about —
  either you are well or you are sick.

If you are well then there is nothing to worry about.

If you are sick there are two things to worry about —
  either you will get well or you will die.

If you get well there is nothing to worry about.

If you die there are only two things to worry about —
  either you will go to heaven or hell.

If you go to heaven there is nothing to worry about.

If you go to hell, you'll be so damn busy shaking
  hands with friends, you won't have time to worry!

Understanding Computer Technology

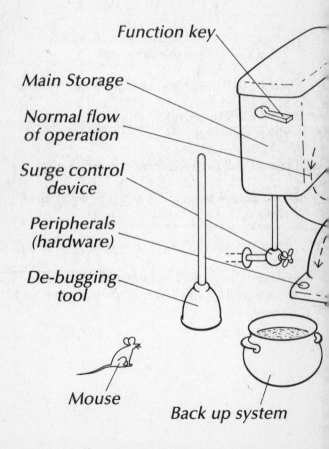

Function key

Main Storage

Normal flow
of operation

Surge control
device

Peripherals
(hardware)

De-bugging
tool

Mouse

Back up system

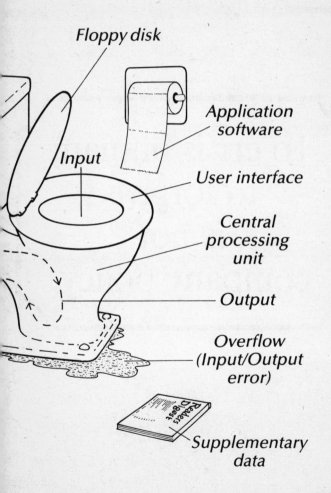

Floppy disk

Application software

Input

User interface

Central processing unit

Output

Overflow (Input/Output error)

Supplementary data

To err is human;
to forgive
is not
company policy.

The lawyer appeals his mistakes;
the doctor buries his;
but the SURVEYOR
monuments and records his.

The good old days

Godliness, cleanliness, and punctuality are the necessities of a good business.

This firm has reduced the hours of work, and the clerical staff will now only have to be present between the hours of 7 a.m. and 6 p.m.

Daily prayers will be held each morning in the main office. The clerical staff will be present.

Clothing must be of a sober nature. The clerical staff will not disport themselves in raiment of bright colours.

Overshoes and top coats may not be worn in the office, but neck scarves and headwear may be worn in inclement weather.

A stove is provided for the benefit of the clerical staff. Coal and wood must be kept in the locker. It is recommended that each member of the clerical staff bring four pounds of coal each day during cold weather.

No member of the clerical staff may leave the room without permission from Mr Rogers. The calls of nature are permitted and clerical staff may use the garden below the second gate. This area must be kept in good order.

No talking is allowed during business hours.

The craving of tobacco, wines or spirits is a human weakness and as such is forbidden to all members of the clerical staff.

Now that the hours of business have been drastically reduced, the partaking of food is allowed between 11.30 a.m. and noon, but work will not on any account cease.

Members of the clerical staff will provide their own pens.

Mr Rogers will nominate a senior clerk to be responsible for the cleanliness of the main office and the private office. All boys and juniors will report to him 40 minutes before prayers and will report after closing hours for similar work. Brushes, brooms, rubbers, and soap are provided by the owners.

The owners recognize the generosity of the new Labour Laws, but will expect a great rise in output of work to compensate for these near Utopian conditions.

Dated 1852 and found in the ruins of a demolished factory in Scotland

Lonesome?
Like to meet people?
Like a change?
Like excitement?
Like a new job?
Just screw up
One more time!

A Short History

COMPLAINT FORM

PLEASE WRITE YOUR
COMPLAINT IN BOX
BELOW. WRITE LEGIBLY.
□

STORES TO BE COMPUTERIZED

"Your pointing at it won't help –
I've still got to find the number on the parts list!"

ACHTUNG!!

Das machine is nicht fur gerfingerpoken und mittengraben. Is easy schnappen der springenwerk, blowenfusen und poppencorken mit spitzensparken. Ist nicht fur gewerken by das dumkopfen, das rubbernecken sightseeren keepen hands in der pockets, relaxen und watch der blinkenlights.

MEMORANDUM

TO: All Managers
FROM: Christmas Chairman
SUBJECT: Decorating Office for Christmas
DATE: 4 December 1990

We have been informed by Whitehall that a White Christmas would be in violation of the Race Relations Act. Therefore, the following steps are to be taken in order to ensure that we comply with the Act during the Christmas season in our offices:

1. All Christmas trees must have at least 23.1 per cent coloured bulbs and they must be placed throughout the tree and not segregated at the back of the tree.

2. Christmas presents cannot be wrapped in white paper. However, interim approval can be given if coloured ribbon is used to tie them.

3. If a manger scene is used, 20 per cent of the angels and one out of the Three Kings must be of a minority race.

4. If Christmas music is played, "We Shall Overcome" must be given equal time. Under no circumstances is "I'm Dreaming of a White Christmas" to be played.

5. Care should be taken in party planning. For example:

   a. Use pink champagne instead of white.
   b. Turkey may be served but only if the white and dark meat are on the same plate. There will be no "separate but equal" plates permitted.
   c. Use chocolate royale ice cream instead of vanilla.
   d. Both chocolate and white milk must be served. There will be no freedom of choice plan. Milk will be served without regard to colour.

A team from Whitehall will visit us on 25 December to determine our compliance with the Act. If it snows on Christmas Eve, we are all in trouble.

An ambitious young typist from Crewe
Thought, "I'll show them just what I can do."
She mastered her Pitman's
And telexing systems
But got stuck on Kalamazoo.

YOU CAN FOOL
SOME OF THE
PEOPLE ALL OF
THE TIME

AND

ALL OF THE PEOPLE
SOME OF THE TIME

A COMBINATION OF
WHICH KEEPS THIS
FIRM GOING.

A SPECIALIST . . .

is someone brought in at the last moment to share the blame

Doing business with you
is like wearing a contraceptive:
One gets a feeling of pleasure
and security whilst being screwed.

I have listened to all your troubles.
Please accept this as a token
of my deepest sympathy.
Then push off.

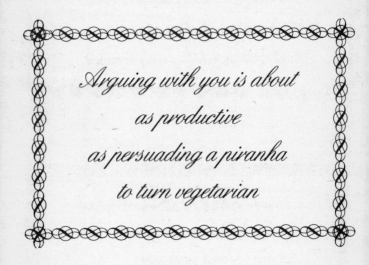

Arguing with you is about
as productive
as persuading a piranha
to turn vegetarian

NOTICE:

As you will know our company has been involved in the formation of a consortium comprising several other large insurance concerns. Accordingly it has been decided to adopt a new coat of arms to represent the new merger.

It is a shield surrounded by laurels, with crossed swords at the top, two lions either side and divided into four, with a man and a woman in bed in each quarter. The laurels represent UNITY, the swords, TRUST, and the lions, STRENGTH. The four couples in bed represent as follows:

1. Man in bed with wife — (LEGAL & GENERAL)
2. Man in bed with girlfriend — (MUTUAL TRUST)
3. Man in bed with secretary — (EMPLOYER'S LIABILITY)
4. Man in bed with prostitute — (COMMERCIAL UNION)

The Board Of Directors

N.B. It has been necessary to add a pram in the centre with a baby's head poking out as we have just bought GENERAL ACCIDENT.

To some people work
is a pain in the neck . . .
however I have a much
LOWER opinion of it.

DON'T TRY TO MAKE A
FOOL OUT OF ME...
I'm doing alright
by myself!

NOTICE!

All employees are requested to take a bath
before reporting for work.
Since I have to kiss your ass to get you
to do anything, I want it to be clean.

Your Supervisor

A GLOSSARY OF STANDARD BUREAUCRATIC TERMS IS
PROVIDED. IT IS HOPED THAT EACH MEMBER OF STAFF
WILL ASSIMILATE THOSE EXPLAINED HERE AND FEEL
CONFIDENT TO USE THEM AT THE CORRECT
JUNCTURE.

It is in process	So wrapped up in red tape that the situation is almost hopeless.
We will look into it	By the time the wheel comes full circle, we assume that you will have forgotten about it too.
A programme	Any assignment that cannot be completed in one phone call.
Expedite	To confound confusion with commotion.
Channels	A trail left by DC's.
Co-ordinator	The bloke who has a desk between two expeditors.
To activate	To make carbons and add more names to the memo.
To implement a programme	Hire more people and expand the office.
Under consideration	Never heard of it.
Under active consideration	We're looking in the files for it.
A meeting	A mass mulling by master minds.
A conference	A place where conversation is substituted for the dreariness of labour and the loneliness of thought.
To negotiate	To seek a meeting of minds without knocking together of heads.

Re-orientation	Getting used to working again.
Reliable source	Bloke you just met.
Informed source	The bloke who told the bloke you just met.
Unimpeachable source	The bloke who started the rumour in the first place.
A clarification	To fill in the background with so many details that the foreground goes underground.
We are making a survey	We need more time to think of an answer.
Note and initial	Spread the responsibility.
Let's get together on this	I'm assuming you're as confused as I am.
See me, or let's discuss	Come down to my office — I'm lonely.
Give us the benefit of your present thinking	We'll listen to what you've got to say as long as it doesn't interfere with what we've already decided to do.
We will advise you	If we figure it out we'll let you know.
Forward for your consideration	You hold the bag awhile.
Approved, subject to comment	Re-read the damned thing.
To give someone the picture	A long, confused and inaccurate statement to a newcomer.

Notice

The objective of all dedicated company employees should be to thoroughly analyse all situations, anticipate all problems prior to their occurrence, have answers for these problems, and move swiftly to solve these problems when called upon . . .

However . . .

when you are up to your ass in alligators, it is difficult to remind yourself that your initial objective was to drain the swamp.

HOW TO SUCCEED WITHOUT TALENT

1. Try to look tremendously important.
2. Don't train yourself to be worthy of promotion; bluff it through.
3. Speak with great assurance but stick closely to generally accepted facts.
4. Avoid arguments, but if challenged, fire an irrelevant question at your antagonist and intently polish your glasses while he tries to answer. As an alternative, hum under your breath while examining your fingernails.
5. Contrive to mingle with important people.
6. Before talking with a man you wish to impress, ferret out his remedies for current problems. Then advocate them staunchly.
7. Listen while others wrangle. Pluck out a platitude and defend it righteously.
8. When asked a question by a subordinate, give him a "have you lost your mind?" stare until he glances down, then paraphrase the question back at him.
9. Acquire a capable stooge, but keep him in the background.
10. In offering to perform a service, imply your complete familiarity with the task, then give it to the stooge.
11. Arrange to be the clearing house for all complaints; it encourages the thought that you are in control and enables you to keep the stooge in place.
12. Never acknowledge thanks for your attention; this will implant subconscious obligations in the mind of your victim.
13. Carry yourself in a grand manner. Refer to your associates as "some of the boys in our office". Discourage light conversation that might bridge the gap between boss and man.
14. Walk swiftly from place to place as if engrossed in affairs of great moment. Keep your office door closed. Interview by appointment only. Give orders by memoranda. Remember, you are a BIG SHOT and you don't give a damn who knows it.

University Hospital

Found on the door of an office.

PRICES	(£ per hour)
Giving advice	10
Taking advice	15
Listening to arguments	25

To: ALL EMPLOYEES (OVER 40)

Re: EARLY RETIREMENT PROGRAMME

As a result of automation as well as a declining workload Management must, of necessity, take steps to reduce the current workforce. A 'Reduction of Employees' programme has been devised which seems the most equitable under the circumstances.

Under the plan, older employees will be placed in early retirement thus permitting the retention of employees who represent the future of the Company.

Therefore, a programme to phase out the older personnel (over 40) by the end of the current financial year will be put into effect immediately. This programme will be known as "RAPE" (Retirement, Aged Personnel, Early). Employees who are "RAPED" will be given the opportunity to seek other jobs within the Company, provided that, while they are "RAPED", they acquire a review of their employment status before actual retirement takes place.

This phase of the programme will be known as "SCREW" (Survey of Capabilities of Retired Early Workers). All employees who have been "RAPED" and "SCREWED" may apply for a final review.

This phase will be known as "STUFFED" (Study of Termination of Use For Further Education and Development).

Programme policy dictates that employees may be "RAPED" once, "SCREWED" twice, but can get "STUFFED" as many times as the Management sees fit.

MANAGEMENT WISHES TO BRING TO THE ATTENTION OF ALL PERSONNEL THE FACT THAT SOME INDIVIDUALS HAVE BEEN USING ABUSIVE LANGUAGE IN THE EXCHANGE OF NORMAL VERBAL COMMUNICATION WITH RELATION TO THE PERFORMANCE OF ROUTINE ACTIVITIES ON THE PREMISES. THIS PRACTICE WILL CEASE IMMEDIATELY.

THE FOLLOWING CODED LIST IS PROVIDED TO PERMIT INDIVIDUAL FREEDOM OF EXPRESSION AND ALLOW ALL THE OUTLET OF FRUSTRATIONS IN A CLEAR CONCISE MANNER. IT WILL PROVE A VERY EFFECTIVE TOOL AND IF EMPLOYED PROPERLY WILL OFFEND NO ONE WITH DELICATE EARS.

To prevent mistaking these communication codes for department numbers and/or telephone extensions, Management has assigned the 900 series numbers to be utilized for your convenience and clarity.

901	COOL IT, THIS IS MY WIFE/HUSBAND. FOLLOW MY LEAD
902	I'M FREE THIS WEEKEND
903	TAKE YOUR TIME. I DON'T WANT TO BE STUCK WITH THIS ASS FOR LUNCH
904	HELP ME UNLOAD THIS MOTHER . . .
905	HEY BABY, LET'S BALL AT LUNCH
906	I'M FREE TONIGHT
907	TIED UP WITH WIFE/HUSBAND TONIGHT
908	MY WIFE/HUSBAND IS OUT OF TOWN
909	LET'S TAKE OFF SICK TOGETHER
910	MEET YOU AT THE MOTEL
911	LET'S TRADE BALLING PARTNERS
912	SORRY DARLING, BUT IT'S THAT TIME
913	WILL SHE OR WON'T SHE???
914	NOPE
915	WHAT A NICE FUCKING BARTENDER
916	BULLSHIT, THE BASTARD SHORT-POURS

YOUR
MOTHER
DOES NOT WORK HERE.

PLEASE PICK UP AFTER
YOURSELF.

ORGANIZATIONAL CHARTS

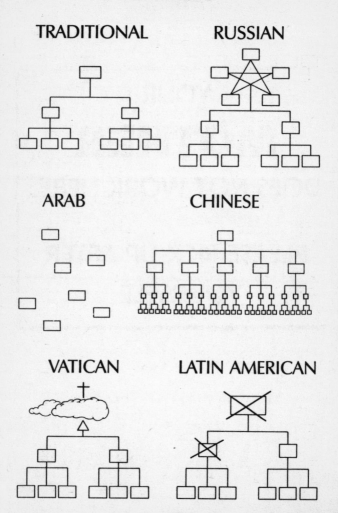

TRADITIONAL

RUSSIAN

ARAB

CHINESE

VATICAN

LATIN AMERICAN

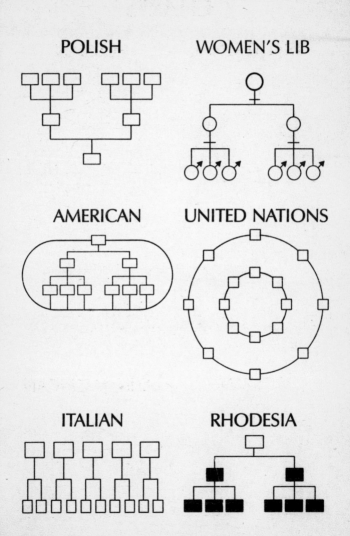

POLISH

WOMEN'S LIB

AMERICAN

UNITED NATIONS

ITALIAN

RHODESIA

45

Notices Strike Back

TRAFFIC ENGINEER'S GUIDE CHART FOR DETERMINING FUTURE TRAFFIC

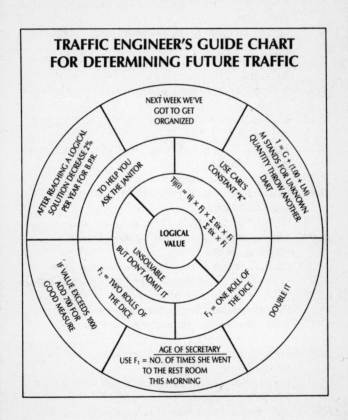

NEXT WEEK WE'VE GOT TO GET ORGANIZED

$I = G + (100 + LM)$ M STANDS FOR UNKNOWN QUANTITY THROW ANOTHER DART

AFTER REACHING A LOGICAL SOLUTION DECREASE 2% PER YEAR FOR B.P.R.

TO HELP YOU ASK THE JANITOR

USE CARL'S CONSTANT "K"

$$Tij(t) = tij \times Fj \times \frac{\Sigma\ tix \times Fi}{\Sigma\ tix \times Fi}$$

LOGICAL VALUE

UNSOLVABLE BUT DON'T ADMIT IT

IF VALUE EXCEEDS 700 ADD 700 FOR GOOD MEASURE

F_2 = TWO ROLLS OF THE DICE

F_3 = ONE ROLL OF THE DICE

DOUBLE IT

$\dfrac{\text{AGE OF SECRETARY}}{\text{USE } F_1 = \text{NO. OF TIMES SHE WENT}}$ TO THE REST ROOM THIS MORNING

EMPLOYEES TIME AND MOTION STUDY
Shop Floor Personnel

7:30	Punched card just as whistle blew.
7:40	Made round of gum machines. No gum. Lost 10p.
8:00	Start looking for tools left around by night shift.
8:10	Find pliers, grind name off and put in my tool box.
8:25	Fellow across room motions to come over. Gives me some gum.
8:35	Go to tool room to tell attendant story. He tells me an old one.
8:55	See foreman coming. Pick up hammer and start pounding.
9:05	Went to toilet. Argued politics with eight other guys there.
9:25	Looked in lunch box to see what wife had packed. Ate banana.
9:30	Match coins with milkman. Drink pint of milk and ate two sandwiches.
9:40	Went to toilet. False alarm.
9:45	Drill hole in piece of metal. Hole too large. Weld hole, start again.
9:50	Go to toilet for smoke. Write name on wall.
10:00	Walk across room to see what other fellows are laughing about.
10:02	Begin to realize that guy gave me laxative gum.
10:03	Go to toilet. False alarm. Sleep for fifteen minutes.
10:20	Plot to get even with other guy.
10:25	Don't need drink but go for one anyway.
10:30	Look for place to hide part made wrong way.
10:35	Can't find any place; toss under partner's bench.
10:37	Look under my bench. Find part made wrong way by night shift.
10:40	Go to foreman and say to him, "look what some guy left under my bench."
10:45	See new female employee; go over and kid with her for fifteen minutes.
11:00	See foreman watching. Pick up 45 pound piece of steel and walk away.
11:02	See freight train going by. Count cars. Bring steel back.

11:20	Realize it's time for lunch. Look in lunch box, remember all eaten, except two meatballs.
11:30	Fix place to sleep on bench.
12:00	Whistle blows. Go to toilet. Draw whiskers on picture on wall.
12:12	Pricked finger on piece of metal.
12:15	Go to first-aid room. Wait in line while nurse takes care of 76 females suffering from old age. Nurse looks at my finger and gives me a vitamin pill.
12:40	Go to cool drink machine for Coke; contact eleven guys for change. Machine empty.
1:15	Go to my machine. See big shot watching. Start taking machine apart.
1:30	Big shot leaves. Can't get it back together.
1:40	Go to toilet. Got in big argument over high taxes.
1:55	Hit finger with hammer while looking at sweater girl. Talked to God.
2:00	Decide to find out who sweater girl is. Walk over, see foreman coming, so go to toilet instead.
2:15	Keep wondering who sweater girl is. Ask six guys. All want to know.
2:17	Assistant foreman coming. Start to study blueprint intently.
2:30	Go to toilet for smoke. Ask nine guys for cigarette. No smoke.
2:40	Go to machine. Some smart alec put grease on all handles.
2:45	Tell foreman this job hurts my back. Want job where I can sit down.
2:55	Knock over full can of rivets. Spent ten minutes picking them up.
3:05	Go to get drink from other department.
3:30	Start cleaning up. Put tools away. Go to toilet. Put on tie.
3:50	Watch out for foreman. Watch out for assistant foreman. Watch out.
3:56	Take apron off. Put on coat. Put apron back with strings untied.
4:00	Whistle! ZIP! Went home. Dead tired.

Next day – same as today – only ask for raise – for merit.

An ARCHITECT is said to be a man who knows very little about a great deal, and keeps knowing less and less about more and more until he knows practically nothing about everything, whereas, on the other hand, an ENGINEER is a man who knows a great deal about very little and who goes along knowing more and more about less and less until finally he knows practically everything about nothing. A CONTRACTOR starts out knowing practically everything about everything, but ends up knowing nothing about anything due to his association with architects and engineers. A SUBCONTRACTOR starts knowing nothing about nothing and never learns anything, as proved by the fact that he continues to do business with architects, engineers and contractors.

Goddam you Charlie Brown.
I WILL NOT SINK IF YOU TAKE IT OUT!

WEIGHT WATCHERS SPECIAL
(How to Lose Pounds
Without Leaving Your Office)

A recent report pointed out that proper weight control and physical fitness cannot be attained by dieting alone. A particular problem is faced by the office person, who spends most of the day behind a desk. Too many of these people fail to realize that hundreds of calories can be burned off, simply by engaging in strenuous exercises that are common for office workers.

The following is a list of calorie-burning activities showing the average number of calories per hour that may be expended:

Beating around the bush	75
Jogging your memory	125
Jumping to conclusions	100
Climbing the walls	150
Swallowing your pride	50
Passing the buck	25
Grasping at straws	75

Beating your own drum	100
Throwing your weight around (depending on weight)	50–300
Dragging your heels	100
Pushing your luck	250
Making mountains out of molehills	500
Hitting the nail on the head	50
Spinning your wheel	175
Flying off the handle	225
Turning the other cheek	75
Wading through paperwork	300
Bending over backward	75
Jumping on the bandwagon	200
Balancing the books	25
Beating your head against a wall	150
Patting yourself on the back	25
Sticking your neck out	175
Racing against time	300
Running around in circles	350
Chewing nails	200
Eating crow	225
Fishing for compliments	50
Climbing the ladder of success	750
Adding fuel to the fire	150
Pouring salt on a wound	10
Wrapping it up at the end of the day	15

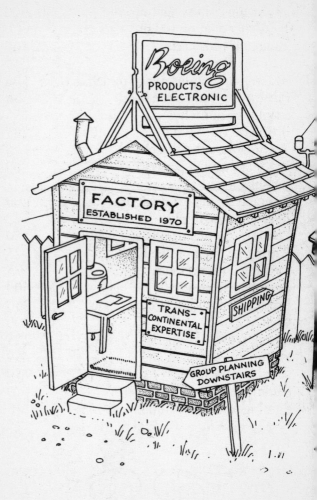

OH SHIT! YOU DID IT
JUST LIKE I TOLD YOU!

PARKING VIOLATION

COUNTY	CAR LICENCE NUMBER

TIME	MAKE OF CAR

This is not a summons, but if it were within my power, you would receive two. Because of your bullheaded, inconsiderate, feeble attempt at parking, you have taken enough room for a 20-mule team, two elephants, one goat, and a safari of Pygmies from the African interior. The reason for giving you this is so that in the future you may think of someone else, other than yourself. Besides I don't like domineering, egotistical or simple-minded drivers and you probably fit one or more of these categories.

I sign off wishing you an early transmission failure (on the motorway at about 4:30 p.m.). Also, may the fleas of a thousand camels infest your armpits.

With my compliments

I am writing in response to your request for additional information. In block number three of the accident report form, I put quote – poor planning – unquote, as the cause of my accident. You said in your letter that I should explain more fully, and I trust that the following details will be sufficient.

I am a bricklayer by trade. On the day of the accident, I was working alone on the roof of a new six-storey building. When I completed my work, I discovered that I had about 500 pounds of bricks left over. Rather than carry the bricks down by hand, I decided to lower them in a barrel by using a pulley which fortunately was attached to the side of the building, at the sixth floor.

Securing the rope at ground level, I went up to the roof, swung the barrel out, and loaded the bricks into it. Then I went back to the ground and untied the rope, holding it tightly to ensure the slow descent of the 500 pounds of bricks. You will note in block number eleven of the accident reporting form that I weigh 135 pounds.

Due to my surprise at being jerked off the ground so suddenly, *I lost my presence of mind* and forgot to let go of the rope. Needless to say, I proceeded at a rather rapid rate up the side of the building.

In the vicinity of the third floor, I met the barrel coming down. This explains my fractured skull and broken collar-bone.

Slowed down only slightly, I continued my rapid ascent, not stopping until the fingers of my right hand were two-knuckles deep into the pulley.

Fortunately, by this time I had regained my presence of mind and was able to hold tightly to the rope in spite of my pain.

At approximately the same time, however, the barrel of bricks hit the ground ... and the bottom fell out of the barrel. Devoid of the weight of the bricks, the barrel now weighed approximately 50 pounds.

I refer you again to my weight in block number eleven. As you might imagine, I began a rapid descent down the side of the building.

In the vicinity of the third floor, I met the barrel coming up. This accounts for my two fractured ankles and the lacerations of my legs and lower body.

The encounter with the barrel slowed me down enough to lessen my injuries when I fell into the pile of bricks and, fortunately, only three vertebrae were cracked.

I am sorry to report, however, that as I lay there on the bricks – in pain, unable to stand, and watching the empty barrel six storeys above me – I again lost my presence of mind and –

I LET GO OF THE ROPE

TO: ALL EMPLOYEES
STREAKING – RULES AND REGULATIONS

IN VIEW OF NUMEROUS ENQUIRIES, THE EMPLOYEES' COUNCIL HAS BEEN ASKED TO STATE THE OFFICE POLICY ON "STREAKING". THE FOLLOWING RULES AND REGULATIONS HAVE BEEN ADOPTED:

1. STREAKING WILL BE PERMITTED AS FOLLOWS:

    A. FEMALE EMPLOYEES WILL STREAK ON ODD DAYS.
    B. MALE EMPLOYEES WILL STREAK ON EVEN DAYS.
    C. ON PAYDAY ALL EMPLOYEES MAY STREAK, SUBJECT TO THE RESTRICTIONS GIVEN IN ITEMS 2 THROUGH 6 BELOW:

2. GIRLS WHO HAVE TATTOOS ON THE LOWER HALF OF THEIR BODIES, SUCH AS "SOCK IT TO ME" OR "WHAT YOU SEE IS WHAT YOU GET", WILL NOT BE PERMITTED TO STREAK (DUE TO THE UNOFFICIAL BULLETIN BOARD REGULATION ON POSTING PERSONNEL NOTICES). MEN WITH TATTOOS, SUCH AS "LET IT ALL HANG OUT" WILL NOT BE PERMITTED TO STREAK FOR LIKE REASONS AS ABOVE. MEN WITH TATTOOS OF BUTTERFLIES, HEARTS AND FLOWERS OR ELVES MUST STREAK WITH THE FEMALES.

3. JUNIOR EXECUTIVES AND FIELD REPS MAY CARRY THEIR BRIEF-CASES WHILE STREAKING. HOWEVER, THE USUAL RULES APPLY. JUNIOR EXECUTIVES MAY NOT CARRY ANY BUSINESS PAPERS, BUT MAY CARRY USUAL ITEMS, SUCH AS A BOX OF KLEENEX, LUNCH, WIFE'S SHOPPING LIST AND PLAYBOY MAGAZINES.

4. GIRLS WITH BUST SIZE LARGER THAN 36B MUST WEAR A BRA WHILE STREAKING IN THE SHOP AREA OR AROUND ANY MOVING MACHINERY. GIRLS SMALLER THAN 36B SHOULD NOT TRY TO IMPRESS PEOPLE BY WEARING A BRA.

5. IF YOU STREAK IN ANY AREA WHERE FOOD IS SERVED, YOU MUST WEAR TWO HAIR NETS. THESE WILL BE AVAILABLE IN THE VENDING MACHINE NEAR THE CAFETERIA DOOR.

6. IN THE EVENT YOUR PHYSICAL MAKE-UP IS SUCH THAT YOUR SEX CANNOT BE DETERMINED, (SUCH AS FLAT CHESTS FOR GIRLS OR LONG HAIR FOR BOYS), YOU MUST WEAR TAGS STATING THAT "I AM A BOY" OR "I AM A GIRL". TAGS WILL BE ATTACHED ON GIRLS WITH A HAIR PIN OR PAPER CLIP; ON BOYS WITH A RUBBER BAND. (NOTE: PLEASE RETURN PAPER CLIPS AND RUBBER BANDS TO THE OFFICE SUPPLY ROOM AFTER YOU FINISH STREAKING.)

STD INSTRUCTIONS FOR USING THE NEW DIAL TELEPHONE

On the telephone there is a dial with letters to indicate the exchange wanted. For instance S for South, P for Portobello or Pussey if using the phonetic code, and O for Operator.

If South is required, put your finger in the P hole for Pussey according to your requirements, and if the Operator is wanted, put your finger in the Operator's hole, and work your finger about until she comes, then she will give you the required connection.

If you have fingered the P hole correctly, you should hear a soft purring sound. Should you have inserted your finger in the wrong hole, the Rs hole for instance, you will hear a high-pitched scream. In this event, discontinue using your finger and put the end of your pencil in Pussey. When you have finished you may find that the Operator has lost her ring.

SPECIAL INFORMATION
Foreign calls may be made by dialling letter F but the girl may require you to use another letter, usually a french letter in addition to the normal procedure.

GENERAL INFORMATION
In certain cases satisfactory connection may prove to be impossible. This could be due to (a) two or more subscribers fingering the Operator's hole at the same time, or (b) the cable engineer's slipped a length in the Operator's socket. You will then have to wait until the engineer has finished using his tool before you can get normal service.

TO REMEDY THE ABOVE FAULTS
(a) Hold your instrument tightly around the middle and feel underneath with your right hand until the Operator responds.
(b) Remove your finger from the P hole or the Rs hole, grasp the flex and pull your wire until you hear a buzzing in your ears.

GENERAL RATE
AND WATER RATES AND CHARGES

Dear Occupier,

I am required to inform you that under Sec. 97 of The Town And Country Planning Act, 1951 (Amended 1964) you are in excess of the water quota allotted to your residence:

97.2   Gallons per month.

The Council Inspector informs us that this is due to over-use of W.C. facilities.

From Jaunary 1990, the extra water will be charged for in the following manner:

A meter will be installed on your W.C. Cistern (if of British Standards design) to register the number of times the W.C. is flushed. The new sliding scale of Water Rates No. 3a are applicable to this installation.

As you are in the first area to come under this scheme you have been allotted 50 FREE FLUSHES of the W.C. after the meter is installed.

Our Department is at your disposal for any problems you may have about this scheme.

I am your obedient servant,

M. E. Dobson

SENIOR SEWAGE STATISTICIAN

PAYMENT BY INSTALMENTS

Any person, other than a Corporation tenant paying an inclusive rent, who is the occupier of a private dwelling may by giving notice in writing to the Borough Treasurer between the 1st February and 30th April in any year elect to pay any rates in respect of his dwelling for the year commencing on the 1st April the same year by ten or less instalments. The convenience of both ratepayers and the Council will be best met if application be made as soon as possible within the period. Once given, the notice will remain effective for subsequent years unless withdrawn by the ratepayer in writing. Upon receipt of such notice the Borough Treasurer will prepare and send to the occupier a statement in writing specifying the number of instalments by which the rates are to be paid in the year in question, the date on which each instalment becomes due and the amount of each instalment.

Should any instalment not be paid by the due date the Borough Treasurer may give notice in writing to the occupier that his notice to pay by instalment is being treated as cancelled, whereupon the whole of the rates due for the current year will become recoverable.

PROFESSORS DO IT WITH CLASS.

Michelangelo did it lying down.

THE POPE DOESN'T DO IT.

The following is a list of accident descriptions received by the MVA from citizens since the Department started recording only serious accidents.

1. Coming home, I drove into the wrong house and collided with a tree I don't have.

2. The other car collided with mine without giving warning of its intentions.

3. I thought my window was down, but I found out it was up when I put my hand through it.

4. I collided with a stationary truck coming the other way.

5. A truck backed through my windscreen and into my wife's face.

6. A pedestrian hit me and went under my car.

7. The guy was all over the road; I had to swerve a number of times before I hit him.

8. I pulled away from the side of the road, glanced at my mother-in-law, and headed over the embankment.

9. In my attempt to kill a fly, I drove into the telephone pole.

10. I had been shopping for plants all day and was on my way home. As I reached the intersection, a hedge sprang up obscuring my vision. I did not see the other car.

11. I had been driving my car for forty years when I fell asleep at the wheel and had an accident.

12. I was on my way to the doctor's with rear end trouble when my universal joint gave way causing me to have an accident.

13. As I approached the intersection, a stop sign suddenly appeared in a place where no stop sign had ever appeared before. I was unable to stop in time to avoid the accident.

14. To avoid hitting the bumper of the car in front, I struck the pedestrian.

15. My car was legally parked as it backed into the other vehicle.

16. An invisible car came out of nowhere, struck my vehicle, and vanished.

17. I told the police that I was not injured, but on removing my hat, I found that I had fractured my skull.

18. I was sure the old fellow would never make it to the other side of the street when I hit him.

19. The pedestrian had no idea which direction to go, so I ran over him.

20. I saw the slow-moving, sad-faced gentleman as he bounced off the bonnet of my car.

21. The indirect cause of this accident was a little guy in a small car with a big mouth.

22. I was thrown from my car as it left the road. I was later found in a ditch by some stray cows.

23. The telephone pole was approaching fast. I attempted to swerve out of its way when it struck the front of my car.

This list has also been submitted to the Bar Association for use by defence attorneys in traffic cases.

APPITUDE TEST

1. If you went to bed at 8 o'clock at night and set the alarm to get up at 9 o'clock in the morning, how many hours' sleep would this permit you to have? _____

2. Do they have a 4th of July in England? _____

3. How many birthdays does the average man have? _____

4. Why can't a man living in Winston-Salem, N.C. be buried west of the Mississippi? _____

5. If you had only one match, and entered a room in which there was a kerosene lamp, an oil heater, and a wood-burning stove, which would you light first? _____

6. Some months have 30 days, some 31. How many months have 28 days? _____

7. If a doctor instructed you to buy three pills, and told you to take one every half hour, how long would they last?
_____

8. A man builds a house with four sides to it and it is rectangular in shape. Each side has a southern exposure. A big bear comes wandering by. What colour is the bear?
_____
Why? _____

9. How far can a dog run into woods? _____

10. What is the minimum number of active baseball players "on the field" during any part of an inning? _____
How many outs make an inning? _____

11. I have in my hand two U.S. coins which total 55¢ in value. One is not a nickel. Please bear that in mind. What are the two coins? _____

12. A farmer had 17 sheep. All but nine died. How many did he have left? _____

13. Divide 30 by ½ and add 10. What is the answer? _____

14. Two men were playing draughts. They played five games and each man won the same number of games. How can you figure this? _____

15. Take two apples from three apples and what do you have?
_____

16. An archaeologist claims he has found some gold coins dated 46 B.C. Do you think he did? _____
Why? _____

17. A woman gave a beggar 50¢. The woman was the beggar's sister, but the beggar is not the woman's brother. How come? _____

18. How many animals of each species did Moses take aboard the Ark? _____

19. Is it legal in North Carolina for a man to marry his widow's sister? _____

20. What word is misspelled in this test? _____

HOW DID YOU SCORE?

16 AND ABOVE: GENIUS

8–15: FAIR

BELOW 8: SUB-NORMAL

Here's to you as good as you are,
And to me as bad as I am,
Yet as good as you are, and as bad as I am,
I'm as good as you are, as bad as I am.

ADDITIONAL ENDORSEMENT

This NCO has an outstanding ability in covering mismanagement and inefficient practices. He is always able to hide things from inspectors and cover obvious errors that normal NCOs would not notice. In several instances he has made the malpractice of the officers in charge of him look like acceptable procedures.

This is a barbell for your pet flea ↦

Dear Marje,

I am writing to you with a problem I am hopeful you can solve. I am married to a sex maniac who thinks of nothing but sex. Everyday when he comes home from work that is the first thing he wants. Even though I am ironing, washing dishes, writing letters

By Appointment to her Majesty the Queen

DR. EPHRAIM LURCH
FENMORE DRIVE
LIVERPOOL, ENGLAND

October 3, 1673

Sir Isaac Newton
189 Wicket Lane
Liverpool, England

Aug. 5   *Emergency treatment of Scalp wound*
caused by falling Apple.

One Guinea

P.S. A most reasonable fee when one
considers the gravity of the situation

I am writing to enquire into the possibility of my having a vasectomy operation. My wife and I have been married for seven years and now have seven children, so you can see that we are now desperate.

We have tried various methods of contraception, all to no avail. We were first advised to try the Rhythm Method but despite trying everything from Waltz to a Rumba my wife still became pregnant and I nearly suffered a permanent injury while trying the Cha-Cha-Cha.

We were also advised to try the "Safe Period" Method and as we were at that time living with in-laws, the only safe time for intercourse was while they were out. Despite this she again became pregnant.

A "Dutch Cap" was the next suggestion but this again we found unsuccessful and an added disadvantage was that despite getting the largest size available my wife found it very tight across the forehead which gave her headaches.

We have also tried a "Sheath" but I had no faith in this from the start despite a demonstration by the Chemist on how to put it on. My wife again became pregnant and I still cannot understand what effect a Sheath rolled on the thumb could possibly have to prevent conception.

The "Pill" also proved useless as it kept falling out until we realized we were using it incorrectly and my wife then held the pill between her knees and this effectively prevented any intercourse at all.

We have tried the "Coil" but found this impossible to use as all the coils are of a let-hand twist and my wife is a right-handed screw. *Coitus interruptus* has been mentioned but we had a very unfortunate experience of this while courting. While performing on the back seat of my car we were interrupted at a most inopportune moment by a patrolling policeman. This resulted in our first pregnancy, only just preceded by our marriage.

As you can understand we are at the end of our tether and if the operation is unsuccessful we shall have to resort to Oral Sex, but what enjoyment there can be in just sitting and talking about it I don't know!

Yours faithfully,

NOTHING
SERIOUS...

... JUST A
LITTLE CHAT
WITH THE
BOSS!

A woman has to
do twice as much
as a man to be
considered half as
good.

Fortunately, it
isn't difficult.

Wife or mother-in-law?

PARTING PUNCHES

Abtholutely Divine

The god Thor had a habit of looking over the countryside for pretty women. He would choose the prettiest. Then at night he would appear in her bed and have his way with her. He never revealed that he was really a god.

Once he found a very beautiful girl, and all during that night he had a marvellous time, the best time ever! It was so good that in the morning he felt he must reward her.

He decided that the best way to show his great favour would be to tell her who he was.

So after an impressive silence, he said, "I'm Thor, darling!"

"Tho am I," she said, "But I'm thatithfied."

SERVE YOURSELF

*No extra charge
will be made*

SIGN IN CHOW HALL

**DUE TO THE LARGE AMOUNT OF
PEOPLE WHO "DON'T GIVE A SHIT,"
EX-LAX HAS BEEN ADDED TO ALL
STAPLES ON THE FOOD LINE.**

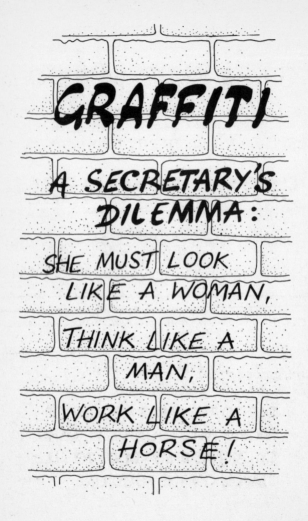

GRAFFITI

A SECRETARY'S
DILEMMA:

SHE MUST LOOK
LIKE A WOMAN,

THINK LIKE A
MAN,

WORK LIKE A
HORSE!

. . . while in this office please speak to me in low, dulcet tones and do not disagree with me in any manner!

. . . understand that when one has reached my age and general state of disillusionment, noise and non-concurrence cause gastric hyper-secretion of the hydrochloric acid, and rupture of the gastric mucosa and . . . I become a most unpleasant bastard.

Bible Belt

TODAY'S PSALM

The union is my shepherd: I shall not work,
It maketh me lie down on the job;
It leadeth me beside the still factories,
It restoreth my insurance benefit.
Yea, though I walk through the shadow of decreased productivity,
I will feel no recriminations,
For the union is with me.
Its restrictive practices, and shop stewards, comfort me.
It prepareth a works committee for me,
In the presence of my employers.
It annointeth my hands with pay rises, my bank balance runneth over.
Surely hire purchase payments and union dues
Shall follow me all the days of my life,
And I shall dwell in a council house forever.

The Reverend Elton Jones
Rescue Mission
Salt Lake City, Utah

Dear Herm,

Perhaps you have heard of me and my nationwide campaign in the cause of temperance. Each year for the past fourteen, I have made a tour of the United States delivering a series of lectures on the evils of drinking. On these tours I have been accompanied by my young friend and assistant Clive Linson. Clive, a young man of a good family and excellent background, is a pathetic example of life ruined by excessive indulgence in whisky and women.

Clive would appear with me at the lectures and sit on the platform drunk, wheezing, staring at the audience through bleary and bloodshot eyes, sweating profusely, picking his nose, belching, passing wind, and making obscene gestures at the ladies, while I would point him out as an example of what over-indulgence can do to a person.

This summer unfortunately, Clive passed away. A mutual friend has given me your name and I was wondering if you would be available to take Clive's place on my 1990 winter tour.

Yours Truly,

Rev Elton Jones

Your Brother in Christ,
Reverend Elton Jones

THE FUND-RAISING PROBLEMS OF
FATHER MURPHY

Father Murphy was a priest in a very poor parish. He asked for suggestions as to how to raise money for his church. He was told that horse owners always had money, so he went to a horse auction but made a very poor buy, as the horse turned out to be a donkey. However, he thought he might as well enter the donkey in a race. The donkey came in third, and the next morning the headlines in the paper read "Father Murphy's Ass Shows". The Archbishop saw the paper and was very displeased. The next day the donkey came in first and the headlines read "Father Murphy's Ass Out Front". The Archbishop was up in arms and decided something had to be done. Father Murphy in the meantime had entered the donkey for the third time, and it came in second. Now the headlines read "Father Murphy's Ass Back in Place". The Archbishop thought this was too much, so he forbade the priest to enter the donkey the next day, which inspired the editor to write "Archbishop Scratches Father Murphy's Ass". When the Archbishop heard this he ordered Father Murphy to get rid of the donkey. Father Murphy couldn't sell it, so he gave it to Sister Agatha for a pet. Now the headlines read "Nun Owns Best Ass in Town". When the Archbishop heard this, he ordered Sister Agatha to get rid of the animal at once. She sold it for ten pounds. Next day the headlines read "Sister Agatha Peddles Her Ass for Ten Pounds". The Archbishop will be buried on Tuesday.

It could have been worse. Suppose the Archbishop had bought 10 per cent of the donkey from Sister Agatha. Imagine the headline "Archbishop Buys Piece of Ass from Sister Agatha".

ORGANIZATION CHART — HEAVEN

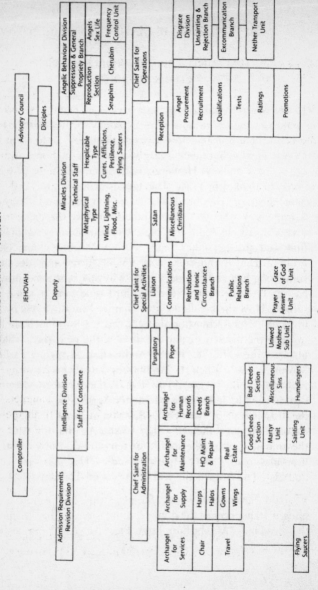

WOE IS MAN

Man is of few days and full of trouble. He laboureth all the days of his youth to pay for a gasoline chariot, and when at last the task is finished, Lo, the thing is junk and he needeth another. He planteth cotton in the earth and tilleth it diligently, he and his servants and his asses, and when the harvest is gathered into barns, he oweth the landlord £8.40 more than the crop is worth. He borroweth money from the lenders to buy pork and syrup and gasoline and the interest eateth up all that he hath. He begetteth sons and daughters and educateth them to smoke cigarettes and wear a white collar, and Lo, they have soft hands and neither labour in the fields nor anywhere under the sun. The children of his loins are cantankerous and one of them becometh a lawyer and another sticketh up a filling station and maketh whoopee with the substance thereof. The wife of his bosom necketh with a stranger and when he rebuketh her, Lo, she shooteth him in the finale. He goeth forth in the morning on the road that leadeth to the city and a jitney smiteth him so that his ribs project through his epidermis. He drinketh a drink of whoopee (!) juice to forget his sorrows and it burneth the lining of his liver. All the days of his life he findeth no parking place and is tormented by traffic cops from his going forth to his coming back. An enemy stealeth his car; physicians remove his inner parts and his teeth and his bank roll; his daughters showeth their legs to strangers; his arteries hardeneth in the evening of life and his heart busteth trying to keep the pace. Sorrow and bill collectors followeth him all the days of his life, and when he is gathered to his fathers, the neighbours sayeth, "How much did he leave?" Lo, he hath left it all. And his widow rejoiceth in a new coupé and maketh eyes at a young sheik that slicketh his hair and playeth a nifty game of bridge. Woe is man! From the day of his birth to the time when the earth knoweth him no more, he laboureth for bread and catcheth the devil. Dust he was in the beginning and in the end his name is MUD.

THE FIRST SERMON

The new priest, at his first Mass, was so afraid he could hardly speak. Before his next service at the pulpit, he asked the Monsignor how he could relax. "Next week," said the Monsignor, "it may help if you put martinis in the water pitcher. After a few sips everything should go smoothly."

That Sunday the young priest put his elder's suggestion to the test and really talked up a storm. After the sermon, he asked the Monsignor how he liked it. The Monsignor replied, "There are a few things you should learn before addressing the congregation again:

1. Next time, sip rather than gulp the martinis.
2. There are ten commandments, not twelve.
3. There are twelve disciples, not ten.
4. David slew Goliath. He didn't kick the shit out of him.
5. We do not refer to our saviour Jesus Christ and his disciples as J C and the Boys.
6. Next week there is a taffy-pulling contest at St Peters, not a peter-pulling contest at Taffy's.
7. We do not refer to the cross as the Big T.
8. The Father, The Son and The Holy Ghost are not known as Big Daddy, Junior and the Spook.
9. Last, but not least, it is the Virgin Mary, not the Mary with the cherry."

Sing a song of Christmas
Office drinking bouts,
Giggling maidens dodging
The drunken plodding louts.

Sing a song of Christmas,
Season that I hate.
Turkey, dressing, pudding
I never should have ate.

Sing a song of Christmas,
Season I detest.
To hell with Red-nosed Rudolph,
Santa, and the rest.

Sing a song of Christmas,
Season I despise.
I only wish the Magi
Had not been quite so wise.

Sing a song of Christmas,
Season that I dread.
All I see before my eyes
Are bows of green and red.

Sing a song of Christmas,
Children's pageant spread
Before the doting parents.
I should have stayed in bed.

Those who think
they know it all
. . . Upset those
of us who do.

*

"You overdid the silicone"

Yea though I walk through
the valley of the shadow
of death I shall fear no evil.
'Cause I am the meanest
'Son of a Bitch' in the valley.

GOD OF THE MONTH CLUB

EACH MONTHLY PACKAGE WILL INCLUDE:
(1) A lavishly illustrated booklet of appropriate prayers and rituals.
(2) Necessary tools and instructions for all prayers and rituals.
(3) Where appropriate, plastic injected graven images are also included.

ALL PACKAGES AIRSHIPPED as some packages will contain foodstuffs such as herbs, herbs with volatile oils, sugar cubes, mushrooms, toadstools (WARNING – please do not confuse these unless you have already applied for your Lifetime Membership), eye of newt, belladonna, etc.

(All Gods and materials authenticated by the Contemporary and Ancient Religions Department of Miskatonic University.)

SPECIAL BONUS FOR JOINING EARLY:
Names of like-minded worshippers in your vicinity! (Correspondence clubs also arranged!)

EXTRA SPECIAL BONUS FOR 5-YEAR MEMBERS:
Group tours chartered to shrines of the month, and other places of interest including: Salem, Stonehenge, Jerusalem, Mecca, Mt. Sinai, etc.

EXTRA EXTRA SPECIAL BONUS! If you agree to take a minimum of two Gods a month, you will receive a SECRET DECODER RING on your birthday, and one sacrifice will be made in your name at God of the Month Club Headquarters.

SPECIAL LIFETIME MEMBERSHIP OFFER:
For those who agree to mention our organization in their wills – send £10 now, plus a photostat of your will, and we will send you an air-mailed, special delivery, gift-wrapped, "Special Jim Jones Package" – please specify Kool-Aide flavour desired. (Offer not available where prohibited by State or Federal Law.)

ADDED BONUS! Special deprogramming services arranged at slight extra charge for those who have fallen afoul of our competition, or those who fear they have got a few months behind. (Courtesy of Ted Kidnap Enterprises, Inc.)

But, you say, "WHAT WILL ALL THIS COST?" Mere pennies! And we guarantee results!

ARE YOU WORRIED ABOUT TITHING TO THE WRONG FAITH?
With God of the Month Club, you'll cover them all! Be in good with ALL deities! Any you can't manage for yourself – (for a slight extra fee) our certified and bonded professionals will do your praying, sacrificing, penances (including lifetime chastity!) for you!!!

(If you should wind up in Hell despite our good services, merely send us an asbestos postcard, and we will cheerfully refund your money! – Minus interest and handling charges of course.)

REMEMBER: The God of the Month Club will bring variety to your life:

Celibacy one month, orgies the next month . . .

A chance to travel to sacred shrines . . .

Companionship with like-minded members . . .

WHAT MORE COULD ANYONE ASK?
Well, we give you more! For 10-Year Members, we offer monthly conferences at our sumptuous headquarters! You, too, can reach true illumination!

DON'T DELAY! TAKE ADVANTAGE OF OUR OFFER TODAY!!!

SPECIAL GIFT SERVICE:
We will send a package of the month, gift-wrapped with a card from you (or "anonymous") to any friend you wish to enrol in the club. (There will be a slight extra charge for enrolling your enemies without their knowledge.)

Dear Earthling,

Hi! I am a creature from outer space. I have transformed myself into this piece of paper. Right now I am having sex with your fingers. I know you like it because you are smiling. Please pass me on to someone else because I'm really horny.

Thanks!

A COMPILATION OF FINAGLE'S UNIVERSAL LAWS FOR NAIVE ENGINEERS

Axiom 1	In any calculation, any error which can creep in will do so.
Axiom 2	Any error in any calculation will be in the direction of the most harm.
Axiom 3	In any formula, constants (especially those obtained from engineering handbooks) are to be treated as variables.
Axiom 4	The best approximation of service conditions in the laboratory will not begin to meet those conditions encountered in actual service.
Axiom 5	The most vital dimension on any plan or drawing stands the greatest chance of being omitted.
Axiom 6	If only one bid can be secured on any project, the price will be unreasonable.
Axiom 7	If a test installation functions perfectly, all subsequent production units will malfunction.
Axiom 8	All delivery promises must be multiplied by a factor of 2.0.
Axiom 9	Major changes in construction will always be requested after fabrication is nearly completed.
Axiom 10	Parts that positively cannot be assembled in improper order will be.
Axiom 11	Interchangeable parts won't.

Axiom 12 Manufacturers' specifications of performance should be multiplied by a factor of 0.5.

Axiom 13 Salesmen's claims for performance should be multiplied by a factor of 0.25.

Axiom 14 Installation and Operating Instructions shipped with any device will be promptly discarded by the Receiving Department.

Axiom 15 Any device requiring service or adjustment will be least accessible.

Axiom 16 Service Conditions as given on specifications will be exceeded.

Axiom 17 If more than one person is responsible for a miscalculation, no one will be at fault.

Axiom 18 Identical units which test in an identical fashion will not behave in an identical fashion in the field.

Axiom 19 If, in engineering practice, a safety factor is set through service experience at an ultimate value, an ingenious idiot will promptly calculate a method to exceed said safety factor.

Axiom 20 Warranty and Guarantee clauses are voided by payment of the invoice.

Axioms 2 and 5 stem from Finagle's more fundamental observation that "The most important leg of any three-legged stool is the one that is missing".

GUARANTEED PERFECT			"HOT-POINT PETER METER"			LAY IT DOWN BOYS		
Just a water spout shoulda been a girl	95% imagination	Seen better days but not many	Just a teaser	Woman's home companion	Secretary's delight	For big girls and small cattle	Old home wrecker size	For bar-room betting only
1	2	3	4	5	6	7	8	9

Due to Numerous Complaints
About Our FREE SERVICE
There Will Be No More
FREE SERVICE

Rebuttal made by Israeli Prime Minister
to United Arab Republic

UNSATISFIED
by Mother Goose?

Georgie Porgie, puddin' n' pie
Kissed the girls and made 'em.

There was a little girl
Who had a little curl
Right in the middle.
You see the damndest things these days!

Jack and Jill went up the hill
To fetch a pail of water.
Jack came down with two black eyes
– A friend of his had lied.

Jack and Jill went up the hill
Each had a buck and a quarter.
Jill came down with two and a half
– They didn't go up for water.

Old Mother Hubbard went to the cupboard
To get her poor daughter a dress.
When she got there, the cupboard was bare,
And so was her daughter, I guess.

Rub-a-dub-dub,
Three men in a tub.
How queer can three guys get?

Twinkle, twinkle, little star,
He took me riding in his car
What we did I ain't admittin'
But what I'm knittin'
Ain't for Britain.

NOBODY IS PERFECT

Each one of us is a mixture of good qualities and some perhaps not-so-good qualities. In considering our fellow man we should remember his good qualities and realize that his faults only prove that he is, after all, a human being. We should refrain from making harsh judgement of a person just because he happens to be a dirty, rotten, no-good son-of-a-bitch!

"I think you should be more explicit here in step two."

Good ol' Sex

What is the difference between a lawyer and an angry hen?
  An angry hen clucks defiance.

What's a kiss?
  Uptown shopping for downtown business.

What's Mother's Day?
  Nine months after Father's Day.

What's a Minute Man?
  A man who double-parks in front of a brothel.

What's virgin wool?
  A sheep that can run faster than the shepherd.

This is his Life

From 20 to 30 – If a man lives right
   It's once in the morning and twice at night
From 30 to 40 – If he still lives right
   He misses a morning and sometimes a night
From 40 to 50 – It's just now and then
From 50 to 60 – It's God knows when
From 60 to 70 – If he's still inclined –

   But don't let him kid you
   It's still in his mind
   His sporting days are over
   His little light is out
   What used to be his sex appeal
   Is now his water spout.
   It used to be embarrassing
   To make the thing behave
   For nearly every morning
   It stood and watched him shave
   But now it's getting older
   It sure gives him the blues
   To have it dangling down his legs
   And watch him clean his shoes.

Amen & Druse

111

Weathermen do it with crystal balls.

You can pick your friends,
And you can pick your nose.
But you can't wipe your friends
On your girlfriend's clothes.

There was a young fellow named Dave,
Who kept a dead whore in a cave.
He said, "I admit
It's a bit of a shit,
But think of the money I save."

Those with short stacks, low manifold pressure or after-
burner malfunction, please taxi up close.

HAND IN HAND,
GLAND IN HAND,
HAND IN GLAND,
GLAND IN GLAND.
BLOODY GRAND!

APARTMENT FOR RENT

A prosperous business man propositioned a beautiful chorus girl. She agreed to spend the night with him for £500. When he was ready to leave, he told her that he didn't have the money with him, but he would have his secretary write a cheque for it and mail it to her calling it "RENT FOR APARTMENT".

On the way to the office the following morning he decided the whole thing wasn't worth the price he had agreed to pay. So he had his secretary send a cheque for £250 and the following note:

Dear Madam:
   Enclosed find cheque for £250 for rent of your apartment. I am not sending the amount agreed because when I rented the apartment I was under the impression that:
   1. It had never been occupied.
   2. That there was plenty of heat.
   3. That it was small.

Last night I found it had been previously occupied, that there wasn't any heat, and that it was too large.

Yours truly,

On receipt of the note the girl immediately returned the cheque with the following:

Dear Sir:
   I cannot understand how you can expect a beautiful apartment to remain unoccupied. As for the heat, there is plenty, if you know how to turn it on. As for the size, it is not my fault that you didn't have enough furniture to furnish it.

Yours truly,

BANANA LOVE CAKE

Ingredients:

2 whole nuts   2 well-shaped legs

1 large banana   2 milk jugs

2 strong arms   1 fur-lined bowl

4 loving eyes

Instructions:

Look into eyes, part legs, gently squeeze milk jugs. Continue until bowl is well greased. Add banana and top with nuts. Move in and out until well creamed. Sigh with relief. Let cool. Do not lick bowl.

Note: If cake starts to rise, leave town.

"Eddie! *Folk* heroes! Your report is supposed
to be on folk heroes!"

TO MY EVER-LOVING WIFE:

During the past year, I attempted to make love to you on 365 individual nights. I succeeded 36 times. This averages once every 10 nights. The following is a list of the reasons you gave me on the nights I didn't succeed:

The children aren't asleep yet	3
We will wake the children	4
It's too hot	11
It's too cold	9
Too tired	33
It's too late	16
It's too early	23
Pretending sleep	56
Window open – neighbours will hear	9
Backache	16
Toothache	2
Headache	10
Giggles	4
I'm too full	4
Not in the mood	22
Baby crying	15
Watched late show	17
Watched early show	15
Mud pack	2
Grease on face	6
Reading Sunday paper	26
Company in next room	7
You're too drunk	5
I'm too drunk	14

Do you think we could improve our record this coming year?

Your loving husband,

You think you have PROBLEMS!

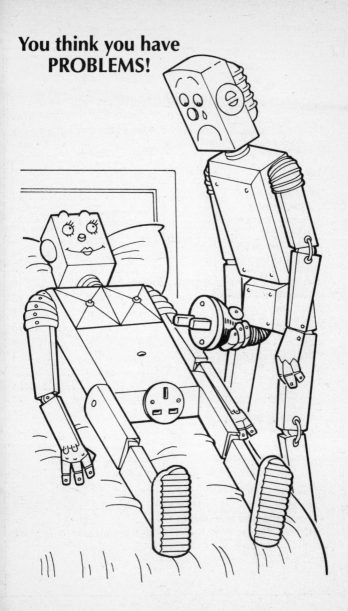

SEXUAL HARASSMENT CONSENT FORM

Name _____   Social Security No. _____

Address _____   Home Phone No. _____

Staff Element _____   Office Phone No. _____

Male _____   Female _____

Sexual Preferences –
  Male–Female   _____
  Female–Female   _____
  Male–Male   _____
  All of the above   _____
  None of the above   _____

I consent to the following forms of sexual harassment –
  Salutatory greetings   _____
  Eye to eye contact   _____
  Eye to bust contact   _____
  Eye below the waist contact   _____

  Heavy breathing on –
    Neck   _____
    Ear   _____
    Other   _____

  Hands on body –
    Shoulder   _____
    Waist   _____
    Gluteus Maximus   _____
    Other   _____

  Feelies   _____
  Gropies   _____
  Penetration, however slight   _____
  Other   _____
  All of the above   _____

MISCELLANEOUS:

I Will _____ I Will Not _____

1. Assist in procurement of various potions, lotions, products, etc., to be used during sexual harassment.
2. Procurement and maintenance of various types of sustaining apparatus.
3. Clean up.

I certify that I will accept sexual harassment from:

Anyone _____

(Attach DOD Directory)

Only _____

(Delete unacceptable names from DOD Directory)

SIGNATURE _____ DATE _____

This form is to be reviewed by immediate supervisor annually, prior to performance rating and updated as necessary.

THE DIETER'S GUIDE TO WEIGHT LOSS DURING SEX

ACTIVITY	CALORIES BURNED

Removing clothes
  With partner's consent 12
  Without partner's consent 187
  Unhooking bra
    Using two calm hands 7
    Using one trembling hand 96

Getting into bed
  Lifting partner 15
  Dragging partner along floor 6
  Using skateboard 3

Achieving Erection
  For normal, healthy man .... 2$\frac{1}{4}$
  For normal, healthy woman 549
  Losing erection .... $\frac{1}{4}$
  Searching for it 115

Putting on Prophylactic
  With erection .... 1$\frac{1}{4}$
  Without erection 300

Inserting Diaphragm
  If the woman who does it is
    Experienced 6
    Inexperienced 73
  If a man does it, regardless of experience 680
  Add 5 calories for retrieving it from across the room

Insertion
  If woman is ready .... $\frac{1}{4}$
  If man is not 274

Positions according to nationality
  Italian: man on top, woman in kitchen 26
  Russian: woman on bottom, man getting permission 55
  American: both on top 60

Possible side effects of intercourse
  Bouncing 7
  Sliding around 9

Serious skidding 12
Whiplash 22

Orgasm
Real 27
Faked 160

Orgasmic intensity scale
Shoes flew off 35
Expression didn't change .... $1/2$
Orchestra swelled 6
Birds sang
   Large birds 7
   Small birds 3
Earth moved 30

Pulling out
After orgasm .... $1/4$
A few moments before orgasm 500

Penis envy
For woman 3
For man 72

Guilt
Despite almost no formal training, orgasm comes
   easily, naturally, and spontaneously 53
You're enjoying sex, despite the fact that other
   people are starving 2
Sex on your lunch hour 3
And you put it on your expense report 20

Aggravation
Partner keeps showing you his/her plants 5
Partner just visited bathroom for seventh time 10
Partner is taking phone calls 7
Partner is making phone calls 40

Getting Caught
By partner's spouse 60
By your spouse .... $60^{1}/2$
Trying to explain 165
Trying to remain calm 100
Leaping out of bed 25
Getting dressed in one large motion 300
Thanking partner quickly 2

PLAYGIRL, LTD
London

Regd. Office PARIS
LONDON
NEW YORK

CENTREFOLD DIVISION

Dear Mr _____

Thank you for your letter and photograph. I regret that we will be unable to use you for our centrefold.

On a scale of 0–10 your body was rated −2 by our panel of women ranging in ages from 60 to 75 years. The panel of widowed and single females rated you −5. We tried to assemble a panel in the age bracket of 25 to 35 years, but we could not control their laughter long enough to get an accurate rating.

The final decision was made when it was discovered that the staples to hold the centrefold 'covered the item of interest'.

Should the taste of our readers ever change so drastically that bodies such as yours are in demand, you will be notified. Meanwhile, please do not call us; we will call you.

Sympathetically,

I. Lovett
Editor
PLAYGIRL LTD

There was a young plumber from Leigh,
Who was plumbing a girl by the sea,
She said "Stop your plumbing, there's somebody coming!"
Said the plumber, still plumbing, "YES ME!!!"

She offered her honour
He honoured her offer
And all night long
He was honour and offer.

A lady swallowed a Blue Gillette, and her doctor
discovered that she had not only given herself a
Tonsilectomy and a Hysterectomy, but she had also
castrated her husband, circumcized her lover, taken
two fingers off a casual acquaintance, given the
Vicar a hare lip and still had FIVE SHAVES left.

IF:
A hat factory girl gets felt three times a day and
A fishmonger displays his cod every morning and
A baker rolls his dough every night and
A miller gets his oats three times a week and
A builder gets an erection every three months and
A jockey gets a ride every Saturday and
A tablecloth gets a jerk off after every meal and
A dentist gets £10 for putting his tool in a girl's mouth –

Why the HELL should a doctor get £25 for coming once?

THE HUSBAND'S CALENDAR
And Why He Goes Astray

SUN.	MON.	TUES.	WED.	THURS.	FRI.	SAT.
OR HOW MANY WAYS CAN YOU SAY NO!!!!		1 I'M OUT OF PILLS!	2 I FORGOT TO TAKE THE PILL	3 I'M TOO TIRED!	4 I HAVE A HEADACHE!	5 IT'S 3 O'CLOCK IN THE MORNING. ARE YOU OUT OF YOUR MIND?
6 IS THAT ALL YOU EVER THINK ABOUT!	7 I'D LOVE TO DEAR, BUT IT'S THAT TIME AGAIN!	8 DITTO	9 DITTO	10 DITTO	11 DITTO	12 IN BROAD DAYLIGHT? YOU BEAST!
13 YOU SHOULD HAVE ASKED LAST NIGHT	14 I'M NOT IN THE MOOD MENTALLY	15 ALRIGHT, I SUPPOSE IT'S MY DUTY!	16 IT'S TOO EARLY!	17 IT'S TOO LATE!	18 IN THE TUB? YOU MUST BE INSANE!	19 NO!!!
20 BEFORE DINNER?	21 I WANT TO WATCH THE LATE SHOW!	22 I'M TOO SLEEPY!	23 NO! AND DON'T GIVE ME THAT HONEYMOON OVER JAZZ!	24 WE DID IT JUST LAST WEEK!	25 DIDN'T I TELL YOU I'M STAYING AT MOTHER'S TONIGHT	26 WHAT DO YOU MEAN WHAT AM I SAVING IT FOR? DON'T TALK NASTY!
27 YOU WANT ME TO WHAT? YOU PERVERT!	28 I SUPPOSE SO BUT HURRY UP IT'S 10:30 ALREADY	29 NO! YOU JUST WANT ME FOR MY BODY!	30 WITH THE LIGHTS ON? WHAT DO YOU THINK I AM?	31 I'VE GOT A CLUB MEETING TOMORROW AND I WANT TO BE RESTED!	BETTER LUCK NEXT MONTH TIGER!!!	

124

WHAT WOULD YOU DO?

A load of coal was being delivered in bags through a customer's garden, and whilst carrying them through the garden the coalman had the misfortune to rub against some washing on the line. The lady noticed this and refused to let him continue the delivery.

Not knowing what to do the coalman phoned his employers as to what he should do. This conversation went as follows:

The lady has her clothes up and I have soiled her knickers with my bags. I have got it half in but she refuses to let me put the rest in, and the half in she refuses to let me take out.

The reply came back:

We realize you are in a hole but reason with her and she might let you put it all in. We would advise you in future to get her permission before you put it in, and ask her to remove all her clothes before you shoot your load.

CONFUCIUS SAY

1. Babies conceived on back seat of car with automatic transmission, grow up to be shiftless bastards.
2. Man who lay girl on hill – not on level.
3. Man who have titty in mouth – make clean breast of things.
4. He who fishes in other man's well – often catch crabs.
5. Wife who put man in doghouse – may find him in cathouse.
6. Boy who play with self – pull boner.
7. Wife who slide down bannister, make monkey shine.
8. Boy who go to bed with sex problem on mind, wake up with solution in hand.
9. Girl who douches with vinegar – walk around with sour puss.
10. Virgin like balloon – one prick – all gone.
11. Girl who go to bed with detective – must kiss dick.
12. Woman who put rooster in freezer – have frozen cock.
13. Man who lay girl in field, get piece on earth.
14. Man who sell Kotex – crack salesman.
15. Blond girl have black hair by cracky.
16. Girl should not marry basketball player – he dribbles before he shoots.
17. Man who screw cook in pantry – sometimes gets ass in jam.
18. Woman who cooks carrots and peas in same pot – very unsanitary.
19. Kotex not best thing in world – but next to it.
20. Man who marries girl with no bust – has right to feel low downs.
21. Man with athletic fingers – make broad jump.
22. Man who play with titty – gets bust in mouth.
23. Squirrel lay on rock and crack nuts – man lay on crack and rock nuts.
24. Woman who fly upside down – have crack up.
25. Man who smoke filter-tip cigarette – sucks titty through nightgown.
26. Woman who springs on innerspring – this spring – get offspring – next spring.

The average time taken by intercourse is four minutes. The average number of strokes per minute is nine. The average number of strokes per intercourse is 36. Therefore the average girl gets 216 inches of peter per intercourse. The average girl gets laid three times per week. That means 3 × 216 = 648 inches or 54 feet of peter per week. A healthy girl averages about 50 weeks per year. There are 5280 feet in a mile, and 54 feet of peter multiplied by 50 equals 2700 feet or just a little over half a mile.

So girls, if you are not getting your half-mile of peter each year, let the man who showed you this help you to catch up.

A young couple, just married, were in their honeymoon suite on their wedding night. As they were undressing for bed, the husband who was a big bruiser, tossed his trousers to his bride and said, "Here, put these on." As she put on his trousers, the waist was twice the size of her body. She said, "I can't wear your trousers." The husband replied, "That's right, and never forget it, because I'm the guy that wears the trousers in this family." With that, his wife flipped her panties to him and said, "Here, try to get into these." He tried to pull them on but couldn't quite make it to his knee-cap and said, "Hell, I can't get in your panties." She said, "That's right, and that's the way it's going to be until your damn attitude changes."

ANTHROPOLOGICAL STAGES OF MAN

IT SEEMS WHEN THE CREATOR WAS MAKING THE WORLD, HE CALLED MAN ASIDE AND BESTOWED UPON HIM 20 YEARS OF NORMAL SEX LIFE. MAN WAS HORRIFIED: "ONLY 20 YEARS?" BUT THE CREATOR DIDN'T BUDGE. THAT IS ALL HE WOULD GRANT HIM.

THEN HE CALLED THE MONKEY, AND GAVE HIM 20 YEARS. "BUT I DON'T NEED 20 YEARS," SAID THE MONKEY. "TEN IS PLENTY."

MAN SPOKE UP AND SAID, "CAN'T I HAVE THE OTHER TEN YEARS?" THE MONKEY AGREED.

THEN THE CREATOR CALLED THE LION AND GAVE HIM 20 YEARS. THE LION SAID HE ONLY NEEDED TEN YEARS. AGAIN THE MAN ASKED, "CAN'T I HAVE THE OTHER TEN YEARS?" "OF COURSE!" ROARED THE LION.

THEN CAME THE DONKEY. HE WAS GIVEN 20 YEARS AND LIKE THE OTHERS SAID TEN YEARS WAS ALL HE NEEDED. MAN ASKED AGAIN FOR THE SPARE TEN YEARS AND AGAIN RECEIVED THEM.

THIS EXPLAINS WHY MAN HAS 20 YEARS OF NORMAL SEX LIFE, TEN YEARS OF MONKEYING AROUND, TEN YEARS OF LION ABOUT IT, AND TEN YEARS OF MAKING AN ASS OF HIMSELF.

Homework

A tramp was leaning against a house close to a window.
Inside he heard voices. Just then he heard a woman explain:

"You simply can't do it that way.
You always let it wobble so you just can't keep it straight.
Not let's try it this way, but be careful of my dress.
If you let it slip out you know you'll make an awful mess.
If you can't do it this way, we can't do it at all.
I think that yours must be too big, or mine, too small.
Just have a little patience, Dear, and you'll surely win.
See, now you got it straight for goodness sake shove it
in."

By this time the tramp had got so excited that he dived for
the window. There he saw a man and woman fitting a pipe
to a stove.

THESE ARE GENUINE EXTRACTS FROM
LETTERS RECEIVED FROM THE GAS BOARD.
COMPLAINTS REGARDING PLACING
APPLIANCES AND METERS, ETC.

"Can you move the meter so it won't cause an obstruction in my passage?"

"The electric man did it through the floorboards, but your man put it in by my front passage where everyone could see it."

"I don't like it as much in the kitchen as I did in the shop window."

LEAKAGES

"Since you put a new pipe from the mains to our house, me and my husband dread going to bed, because of a slight discharge. We think there is a leak just after it enters."

"I told my husband it was safe to leave it in all night, but he won't. If he comes to the showroom like I did, can the lady satisfy him behind the counter and talk him out of it."

GENERAL

"I was told mine is no good but if it is altered I can get the North Sea in."

"I have heard there are two ways you can have it and it worked out cheaper the more you got if you have it the other way."

"I am not satisfied with an apprentice so will you send a man to do it properly."

"My wife will be ready for your man if you will let her know when he is coming on a postcard."

"I will try to pay before the end of the month, because my husband will be surprised if you cut it off without telling him."

"My husband is pretty handy, but he says your men can do it better because of their tools."

"It has gone slack with use, and my husband can't make it tight, no matter how he tries, so for the time being we are making do with an old gas ring."

"My slot is not blocked now, but your men made an awful mess in banging their tools on the wall."

"Since I made the arrangements with your salesman I am having a baby and would like to change it for a drying cabinet."

"My neighbour has a bigger one than I had, it makes a difference to her water when she fills the bath."

"My husband was under the impression I was getting it at a reduced rate but your salesman didn't use his head and got me into trouble."

"It is about time your workman came back to fill the hole because we are fed up of having it in the street, it is a big attraction and we are getting children by the dozen."

"The woman who is after the house says she is not keen on it, so if she gets it can your man stand by to take it out before she comes."

WHY CUCUMBERS ARE BETTER THAN MEN

The average cucumber is at least six inches long.
Cucumbers stay hard for a week.
A cucumber never suffers from performance anxiety.
Cucumbers are easy to pick up.
You can fondle a cucumber in the supermarket.
And you know how firm it is before you take it
    home.

Cucumbers can get away any weekend.
A cucumber will always respect you in the morning.
A cucumber won't ask: Am I the first?
Cucumbers won't tell other cucumbers if you are a
    virgin.
With cucumbers you don't have to be a virgin more
    than once.

Cucumbers don't have any sex hang-ups.
You can have as many cucumbers as you can handle.

You only eat cucumbers when you feel like it.
Cucumbers don't ask:
. . . Am I the best?
. . . How was it?
. . . Did you come?
. . . How many times?

Cucumbers don't mind hiding in the refrigerator
    when your mother comes over.
A cucumber will never make a scene because there
    are other cucumbers in the refrigerator.

Cucumbers don't come in your mouth.
No matter how old you are, you can always get another cucumber.
A cucumber will never give you a lovebite.
Cucumbers can stay up all night and you don't have to sleep on a wet spot.
Cucumbers won't leave you wondering for a month.
Cucumbers won't tell you a vasectomy will ruin it for them.
A cucumber doesn't forget to flush the toilet.
A cucumber doesn't flush the toilet when you are in the shower.

Cucumbers don't compare you to a centrefold.
Cucumbers don't tell you they liked you better with long hair.
A cucumber will never leave you for:
. . . another woman
. . . another man
. . . another cucumber.

You always know where a cucumber has been.
Cucumbers don't have mid-life crises.
Cucumbers don't play the guitar and try to find themselves.
Cucumbers never expect you to have little cucumbers.
It's easy to drop a cucumber.
No matter how you slice it, you can have your cucumber and eat it too.

Dear Friend:

This chain letter started with the hope of bringing relief and happiness to all tired husbands or boyfriends.

Unlike most chain letters, this one does not cost money. Simply send a copy of this letter to six of your married or almost hitched acquaintances, who are equally tired. Then bundle up your wife or your girlfriend and send her to the man at the top of the list.

When your name comes to the top of the list, you will receive 16,487 women and some will be dandies. Have faith in this letter, one man broke the chain and got his old lady back. Don't let this happen to you.
Sincerely,
A Good Friend

PS: At the time of writing, a good friend of mine had received 36 women. They buried him yesterday, and it took seven undertakers 36 hours to the wipe the smile off his face.

GRAMMAR AS WROTE

Dear Sir,

you never past me in grammar because you was prejudice but I got this here athaletic scholarship any way. Well, the other day I finely got to writing the rule's down so I can always study it if they ever slip my mind.

1. Each pronoun agrees with their antecedent.
2. Just between you and I, case is important.
3. Verbs has to agree with their subjects.
4. Watch out for irregular verbs which has crope into our language.
5. Don't use no double negatives.
6. A writer mustn't shift your point of view.
7. When dangling, don't use participles.
8. Join clauses good, like a conjunction should.
9. Don't write a run-on sentence you got to punctuate it.
10. About sentence fragments.
11. In letters themes reports articles and stuff like that we use commas to keep a string of items apart.
12. Don't use commas, which aren't necessary.
13. Its important to use apostrophe's right.
14. Don't abbrev.
15. Check to see if you any words out.

DID YOU HEAR ABOUT . . .

The window cleaner who scared the boss right out of his secretary.

The recent cigarette survey that disclosed that 99 per cent of the men who have tried Camels have gone back to women.

The farmer who couldn't keep his hands off his wife so he fired them.

The nurse they thought had drowned until they found her under the doc.

The little boy that found a 50 pence piece. so he went home for some money.

The new rule at the girl's school ... lights out by ten. candles by eleven.

The drunken midget who walked into a home for girls and kissed everybody in the joint.

She's fine, understanding ... and wonderful laying down too.

The meanest man in the world didn't tell his wife he was sterile until she got pregnant!

The over-eager bride who came, walking down the aisle.

The real smart girl who could play post office all night without getting any male in her box.

The sultan who had ten wives. Nine of them had it soft.

What to do about fall-out. Re-insert and shorten the strokes.

Where cousins come from? Ant holes.

The new vitamin made from chicken blood makes men cocky and women lay better.

Witches don't have babies because their husbands have Holloweenies.

Cuddle up a little closer. it is shorter than you think.

If sex is a pain in the ass for you ... you are doing it wrong.

The fastest four-handed game in the world is when it slips out.

She was a farmer's daughter. but she couldn't keep her calves together.

The French soldier who kissed both his wife's cheeks before he went to the front.

She said she would do anything for a mink coat; she got one, and now she can't button it.

The fellow who got ten years for pumping Ethyl behind the station.

The fellow who chased his girlfriend up a tree and kissed her between the limbs.

NOTICE TO CALLERS

Friendly calls .... 10 minutes
Salesmen, with 'Real deals' .... Half second
Life Insurance Agents .... 15 seconds
Liquor Salesmen, with samples .... 2 hours
Friends letting us 'in on the ground floor' .... 1 second
Friends inviting us to lunch .... 2 hours
Friends wishing to talk hunting/fishing ... Most of the day
Those wishing to pay bills .... All day
Customers .... 8 hours
Wives .... No time
Girlfriends .... All night
Wealthy relatives in their 80s .... Any time
Relatives wanting jobs .... 3 seconds
Bill and Tax Collectors .... All day (tomorrow)

TURKEY STUFFING
10–17 Lbs

4 Cups Breadcrumbs
2 Eggs
1 Teaspoon Salt
1 Onion (chopped)
$\frac{1}{2}$ Cup Diced Celery
1 Cup *Uncooked* Popcorn

Mix ingredients and stuff turkey. Bake in moderate oven (325 degrees fahrenheit) for four hours. After four hours get the hell out of the kitchen because the popcorn will blow the ass right off the turkey.

SWINGERS

A couple decided to celebrate their tenth anniversary by inviting another couple, their closest friends, to make a real night of it with them.

They booked into a big hotel, had a smashing meal and plenty to drink, and then the husband suggested that they take a flyer and gamble a bit. None of them had ever tried it before, but they discovered that they enjoyed it very much.

Then the husband said, "If you're all game for another novelty, how about changing partners? Just for this one night?"

They had some more to drink, and then they all agreed. The exchange took place.

The next morning the husband woke up. He said, "You know that was terrific! Marvellous! Tremendous! I've never known it could be like that!"

Then a little later he said, "I wonder how the girls are making out."

UNIVERSITY CURRICULUM

Term I: *Introduction to Nose-Picking*

Term II: *Abnormal Nose-Picking*

Term III: *Applied Nose-Picking*

Term IV: *Individual Nose-Picking Differences*

Term V: *Introduction to Plastic Surgery*

GVPT 100   – Political Theory, Machiavelli to the
                Corner Grocer
PHIL 110   – How to Ask Lots of Questions and
                Appear Intelligent
                Text: Plato as taught by Socrates
SPEECH 310 – Political Speechmaking through Use
                of Buzz Phrase Generator
BUS 400   – Ambiguous Bills
ECON 410   – Use of GNP as Index of National
                Wealth and Other Jokes
LAW 480   – Torts and Other Bitches

Celebrations!

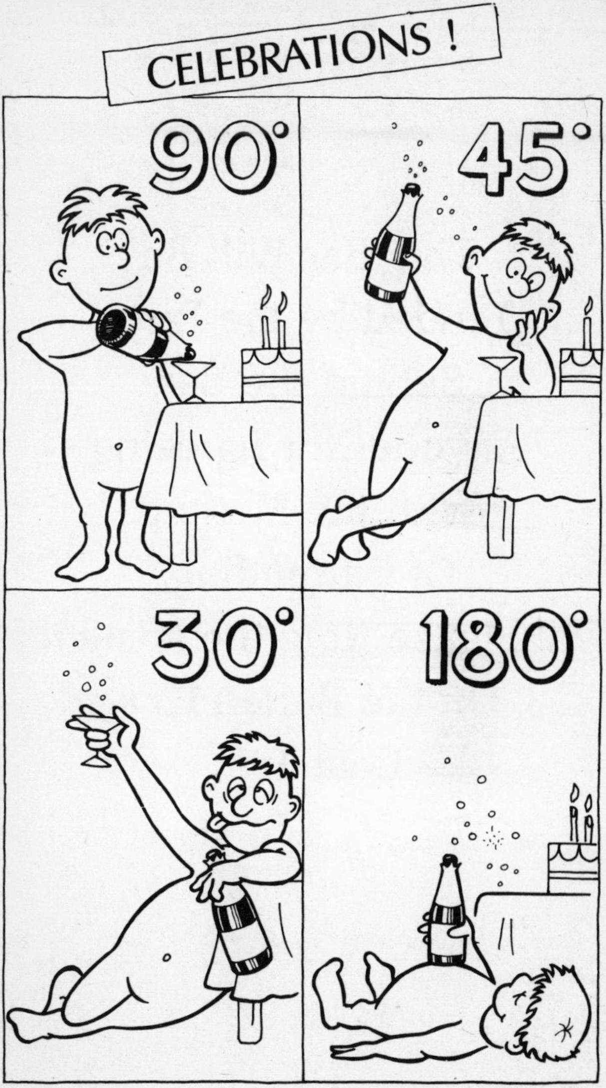
CELEBRATIONS !
90°
45°
30°
180°

This Bar Will Be
Tended by the Party
Behind the Bar.
Anyone Not Agreeing
With the Method
Of Bartending,
Will Please Note the Mistletoe
On the Bartender's
Coat Tail.

RULES AND REGULATIONS
FOR PARTY GUESTS

IF THE BATHROOM IS OCCUPIED, YOU MAY USE THE SINK

You can get a drink of water there, as easily as you can in the bathroom.

WE WANT YOU TO FEEL AT HOME. IF YOU FEEL SICK, YOU WILL FIND A BUCKET UNDER THE TABLE

Often ducking one's head into a bucket of cold water will revive one quickly.

"EVERYTHING FOR YOUR CONVENIENCE" IS OUR MOTTO. IF CONVERSATION LAGS, START TALKING POLITICS

All our neighbours are sitting up waiting for a fight to start, and we don't want to disappoint them.

IF YOU WANT TO NECK – HOP TO IT LAY YOUR HATS (AND WHAT YOU BROUGHT WITH YOU) ON THE BED. WE'RE NOT SUPERSTITIOUS

Everything but the kitchen stove has been laid on it.

IF YOUR FEET HURT, TAKE OFF YOUR SHOES

Nothing bothers us, as we were born next door to a glue factory.

IF YOU PLAY POKER
Take her out in the back yard. Don't wreck our furniture!

IF YOU PLAY BRIDGE
Remember, "Painless Sparker" has to live too. Knock out someone's teeth.

IF YOU PLAY BLACK JACK
You will find a dandy in the table drawer. It's loaded with buckshot.

IF YOU PLAY SOLITAIRE
You should be ashamed of yourself!

MEN WILL KISS THE HOSTESS GOODNIGHT. WOMEN WILL KISS THE HOST

This will give us something to fight about after you're gone.

IF YOU HAVEN'T A CAR TO TAKE YOU HOME, TAKE OURS

The loan company is going to take it next week anyway.

OFFICE PARTIES

My Very Dear Friends:

When I came into the office this morning I noticed a sort of general attitude of unfriendliness and since several of you have openly called me a dirty son of a bitch to my face, I seem to get the feeling that I must have done something wrong at our office party last Friday. The Manager called me today from the hospital and as this is evidently my last day, I would like to apologize to all of you. I would like to speak to each of you personally but you all seem to go deaf and dumb when I try to talk to you.

First, to our beloved boss, Mr. Cone. I am truly sorry for all the things I called you. I am aware that your father was not a baboon nor your mother a Chinese whore. My story of buying your wife for fifty pence was strictly a figment of my imagination. Your children are undoubtedly yours too. I feel badly about the water cooler incident and I hope it didn't hurt your head when they took the jug off. My sincere regrets to comely Miss Ashby. In my defence I believe that you enjoyed the little escapade on the stairway until the banister broke and we fell to the second-floor landing. In spite of the damage which occurred when we landed, I am sure that you will admit that it was one of the greatest thrills that you ever had.

Sam Franklin, you old cuss, you've got to forgive me for the little prank I played on you. I didn't know you were so goosey but it might have been a lot worse if that fat lady hadn't been standing right under the window when you jumped through. She broke your fall. People have been killed falling that far.

Mr. Gray, I regret telling the firemen that you caused the false alarm, but I really didn't think they would be such bad sports about it. Those fire hoses sure have a lot of force, don't they? I had no idea they would turn that cold water on you.